NAHUM, HABAKKUK & ZEPHANIAH
BIBLE STUDY
BSBP SERIES
(Bible Studies for Busy People)

Margaret Weston is the author of 'How do I know I know God?' a best seller in Christian Evangelism and the first book in the 'How do I know?' series. She is also the author of the BSBP series. Full details can be found at www.howdoiknowbooks.com

All profit made by the author from this book is donated to Tearfund.

Tearfund is a Christian international aid and development agency working globally to end poverty and injustice, and to restore dignity and hope in some of the world's poorest communities.

Tearfund operates in more than fifty countries around the world. As well as being present in disaster situations and recovery through their response teams, they speak out on behalf of poor people on the national and international stage by petitioning governments, campaigning for justice and raising the profile of key poverty issues wherever they can. Find out more at www.tearfund.org

ISBN-13: 978-1516995493
ISBN- 10: 151699549X

BIBLE STUDY (BSBP SERIES) FOR THE BOOKS OF NAHUM, HABAKKUK AND ZEPHANIAH

CONTENTS

BSBP SERIES
(BIBLE STUDIES FOR BUSY PEOPLE)

The world is becoming increasingly busy and as Christians we are not immune from this. There always seems to be so much to do but so little time to do it! However, many of us love the Bible and would like to have more time to study it. So............

The BSBP series has been prepared just for people like us – those who have a real desire to study the Bible but find they simply do not have enough time.

Do you want to study the Bible? Have you been put off by the length - and depth - of many of the books that are on offer? If your answer is 'yes' to these questions then the BSBP series is for you!

You will be taken step by step through your chosen book of the Bible - just 10 studies with 10 questions in each study. The brief supporting notes, will keep you focused on the job in hand. You will quickly and easily get a sound grasp of the subject matter - without having to use hours and hours of your valuable time!

These studies are ideal for both personal study and for stimulating thoughtful discussion within small groups.

The supporting notes roughly follow the order of the questions in each study. The best way to use the study is to first read the Bible section and prayerfully consider the questions. The notes can then be used either after each question to help stimulate thoughts or discussion, or when each study has been completed.

If you have any comments I would love to hear from you. You can find contact details on the following website: www.howdoiknowbooks.com

May God bless you as you study His Word and by so doing increase in your knowledge of Him.

Nahum
Background and Introduction

Nahum, Habakkuk and Zephaniah were all prophets at a similar time in the history of Israel i.e. between 650BC and 600BC approximately. In 722BC the Assyrians had invaded and destroyed the northern kingdom of Israel and in 701BC they invaded Judah (see 2 Kings 17:6 and 18:13-18.) At this point in history Assyria was drunk with power and wealth. She would not acknowledge her sin or listen to God.

The book of Nahum is a prophecy against Nineveh. Whilst many people will know of Jonah and his message for Nineveh, perhaps Nahum is less well-known. There is a significant difference between the response of Nineveh to the message of Jonah, and its response to Nahum.

Jonah prophesied the destruction of Nineveh but the people listened and repented. Thus God did not destroy them. Jonah was somewhat annoyed that God did not bring about the destruction he had prophesied! But when we – or Nineveh – turn to God in repentance, He is willing to forgive. Thus, He did not at that time destroy Nineveh.

However, when Nahum prophesied against this great city, the people refused to repent of their great wickedness. Therefore, Nahum's prophecy came true and we know from history that the judgment of God fell on Nineveh. It was razed to the ground.

Nineveh was one of the oldest and greatest cities in antiquity and was the largest city in the world for around 50 years. Sennacherib (king of Assyria 705BC-681BC) made Nineveh a huge magnificent city (around 700BC) but he was a wicked man and it seems he was eventually murdered by one of his own sons.

Nineveh was however razed to the ground around 612BC by allied forces which included the Babylonians, Chaldeans, Medes and Persians. It was never rebuilt again. Thus the prophecy of Nahum against Nineveh came true.

The name Nahum actually signifies 'a comforter' which is surprising given the severity of his message. But even though his message speaks terror to the Assyrians, it would have brought comfort to the ten tribes of Israel who had been carried captive into Assyria.

Many Bible scholars believe that the first chapter of Nahum was written some years before the second and third. His words would have been an encouragement to Israel after they had been captured by the king of Assyria. It is thought that chapters 2 and 3 were written much nearer to the time when Nineveh was conquered.

Today the ruins of Nineveh are across the river from the modern day city of Mosul in Iraq.

In Nahum we learn more about the great God we know. This book is perhaps particularly relevant for the world in which we live today. There is so much evil in the world, just as there was here in Nineveh. Our God is patient and today He is still waiting for men and women to repent and turn to Him, so that His wrath and judgment do not fall on them, as it did on the Ninevites. But we must also remember that He will not be patient forever, and time is running out. Our God is One who 'will not leave the guilty unpunished' (Nahum 1:3) but who will one day judge the wickedness and evil that there is in our world.

Study 1 – Chapter 1 (Nahum)
The Lord's anger against Nineveh

Discuss/think about

What do you think about when you think about God? A.W. Tozer says, "What comes into our minds when we think about God is the most important thing about us."* Think about/discuss some of the characteristics/attributes of God.

Read Nahum chapter 1

1. What similarities are there between Jonah and Nahum?

2. Why did God not do what He said He would do when Jonah preached destruction against Nineveh?

3. We know from history that God did judge Nineveh after Nahum's prophecy against it. So why did God not act in judgment after Jonah prophesied, but He did after Nahum prophesied?

4. What does this tell us about God's character, that we can apply to our own lives?

5. Think of some of the cities of the world where evil is rampant. What do you think would happen if a similar message was preached to them, as the one that Nahum preached to Nineveh?

6. Do you find the first 8 verses of this chapter comforting or terrifying? Discuss why you feel as you do.

7. If we know Jesus, how does this help us to interpret verse 3 (1:3)?

8. Read 2 Peter 2:22 and Hebrews 10:26. How do these verses apply to Nineveh? How might they apply to us today?

9. Which verses in this chapter could be a reference to the Good News about Jesus?

10. What strikes you most about this opening chapter of Nahum?

Don't forget to pray

Ask God to help you remember that He is just and holy which is part of His love. Ask the Holy Spirit to help you remember how much God hates sin, and ask for His help to live in a way that pleases God. Thank the Lord Jesus for taking the punishment we deserved, when He died on the cross.

* The Knowledge of the Holy by A.W. Tozer

Nahum Chapter 1- Notes

We see many characteristics of God portrayed in this chapter. Perhaps we don't like to think of God as a 'jealous and avenging' God. Maybe we don't like to think about His vengeance and wrath. But in this chapter we see a magnificent display of the glory of God. We see His wrath and justice against the wicked, and we also see His mercy and grace towards those who trust in Him. We also see His great majesty and power, shown towards both good and evil. It is helpful to study such books as Nahum and other prophets in order to understand more about the character of God.

The character of God never changes. The God of the Old Testament is the same God of the New Testament. We know a God of love but what kind of love would it be if it was not also just? What kind of love would it be if wickedness was not eventually punished and banished for ever? And so we see Nahum warning Nineveh about the coming judgment of God because of the wickedness there. Genesis 6:3 (NKJV) says, 'My Spirit shall not strive with man forever…'

Nahum and Jonah preached a similar message to Nineveh. The Ninevites had listened to the message of Jonah and repented. But now their hearts had become hard and they had turned back to their sin. So the result could only be judgment.

This book contains a solemn warning to us today. We cannot trifle with God. If we love and trust Him, then we can lean on the promises in 1:7-8. But if we refuse His love and insist on continuing with our sinful ways, we can only expect judgment.

When we think of the evil that seems to be gaining the ascendancy in many parts of the world, we can rest assured that God sees this and remains in control. He will not allow it to go on forever, and one day He will judge. So it is a comfort to understand that 'the Lord will not leave the guilty unpunished.' Today we don't hear of whole cities coming to God in repentance, but we do hear of many individuals. We know that in many places the good news about Jesus is reaching many people. We also hear of many accepting

Jesus into their lives after seeing visions and having dreams about Him. God is not limited and can speak in many ways. He is also patient which is why the Day of Judgment has not yet come.

We do well to 'fear' God in the sense of having a right respect and reverence for Him. But because of His great love we can also know Him as 'our Father'. So when we read of judgment we do not need to be terrified, if we know God through the Lord Jesus Christ.

We read in 1:3 that 'the Lord will not leave the guilty unpunished'. We know that sin must be punished. But we can praise and thank God because we can also know that Jesus took our punishment when He died on the cross for us.

We can see how 2 Peter 2:22 and Hebrews 10:26 could apply to the Ninevites. They had repented when Jonah had preached judgment. God had accepted their repentance and had not carried out the terrible things that Jonah prophesied against Nineveh. But they had turned back to their sin. They had, in effect, trampled on God's goodness and mercy. This time they would find that God would indeed do exactly what He said He would do, as prophesied by Nahum.

Hidden in a message containing such dire warnings, we find beautiful references to the good news about Jesus. Even in such a dark time, there was hope. Verses 7 and 15 are shining out in the darkness. There is hope for those who trust in God. There is One who is coming who will be bringing good news of salvation for mankind. One who is coming to reconcile God and man. One who is bringing 'peace and good will'. ***"Glory to God in the highest, and on earth peace, good will toward men."*** Luke 2:14 (NKJV). His name, of course, is JESUS!

Study 2 – Chapter 2 (Nahum)
Nineveh to fall

Discuss/think about

How do you feel when you hear other people blaspheme? Do you speak out or do you remain silent? Why/why not?

Read Nahum chapter 2

1. Why do you think the prophet Nahum speaks in this chapter in the present tense? In other words, he is speaking as if these events are actually happening.

2. How would you feel if similar things were said against your town or city?

3. Why is there no doubt that these things will happen to Nineveh?

4. Why do you think the Ninevites ignored Nahum and did not repent? (Even though they had done so previously when Jonah prophesied disaster.)

5. Do you think many people today believe in God's judgment? Do you?

6. How could we be similar to the Ninevites today?

7. What do you think is meant by the reference to the lions in 2:11?

8. What do you think is meant by the last verse of chapter two – 'The voice of your messengers will no longer be heard'?

9. Why is God justified in all that He intends to do against Nineveh?

10. Why and how does God warn us sometimes about our actions?

Don't forget to pray

Ask God to help you understand more about His judgment, so that you will be more urgent in telling others the good news about Jesus.

Nahum Chapter 2 – Notes

We read in chapter 1 that, 'the Lord is a jealous and avenging God; the Lord takes vengeance and is filled with wrath'. Perhaps if we remembered this we would be more willing to say something when we hear others blaspheme. We know God is not willing that any should perish (2 Peter 3:9), but we also know that God is not mocked (Galatians 6:7). The judgment that Nahum pronounces on Nineveh does come, because the people refused to listen to God. He had already shown His goodness when they repented following Jonah's message. Therefore, they knew He would do the same if they repented and turned from their wicked ways. But they refused to listen. This is a solemn message for us today.

Nahum speaks of these events as if they are happening because he knows there is no doubt. God has spoken, therefore, the events are as sure to happen as if they were actually happening now. We too can be sure of God's Word. If He has spoken, it will happen just as He has said.

We might think it strange that there was no repentance in Nineveh. The Ninevites would have known about Jonah's message and what had happened then, because it had occurred in fairly recent history (about 150 years before). Why then, did they not turn back to God and thus escape the judgment? We might ask similar questions today. Do we learn from history?

We can see how many become hard in their mind and attitude against God and the good news about Jesus. Pride was probably at the root of the problem in Nineveh. Sennacherib had made Nineveh a huge and magnificent city and it was the largest city in the world for around 50 years. How easily humankind fall into the trap of pride. So proud of their achievements and success, so proud of their scientific discoveries, but forgetting about their Creator!

Many people today do not believe in a God of judgment. And many of the same people ask why God allows so much suffering! We must be careful not to think that because God is love, He will not judge or punish anyone. Some say that a loving God would not send people to hell. But this is to misunderstand love. How can true love allow sin and evil to continue to spoil everything for ever? Although God is patient, He must deal with evil *because* He is a God of love. Most of us become angry if we see those who kill and steal not punished.

The Assyrians were known for their cruelty. They had become absolutely brutal in their conquests. Apparently they would hang the bodies of their victims on poles and use their skins on the walls of their tents! The reference to the lions is probably referring to the princes and nobles of Nineveh. They were proud and cruel and everyone stood in awe of them. But the Lord is against them and the sword will devour them. However great human kings and nobles think they are, however revered they are by others, God is so much greater and no-one can stand in the way of His plans and purposes.

Many scholars believe that the reference to the messengers in the last verse of chapter two refers to Rabshakeh. He was one of Nineveh's messengers that had blasphemed the living God. This was a great sin which was remembered against Nineveh for a long time after. However, we don't know this for sure. It could mean that there would no longer be any messengers speaking to them about God. There will be a day coming in this world too, when the gospel message will no longer be preached. This makes it all the more urgent to warn people, in love, today.

God is always just in all that He does. There is always a consequence for sin. It may appear that God overlooks evil, but He never does. And the Bible makes it very clear that one day evil will be judged completely and banished forever. Nahum was telling the people of Judah not to despair, because God had pronounced judgment. Soon these cruel people would be getting just what they deserved. This should bring comfort today to Christians who are persecuted and suffer under extreme cruelty. God does not overlook this. Judgment will come.

God often does warn us about our actions because of His great love. He is not willing that any should perish but our salvation must be on His terms, not ours.

Study 3 – Chapter 3 (Nahum)
Reconciliation

Discuss/think about

How do you feel about the terrible atrocities that are being carried out in our world today? How do you feel about the men and women who do these terrible things, or who support those who do?

Read Nahum chapter 3

1. List some of the awful sins that are mentioned in this chapter. Can you identify any specific place in the world where these things are happening today?

2. Do you think God feels any differently today about these awful atrocities, when comparing the situation with His feelings about Nineveh?

3. God pronounces judgment on Nineveh, and then carries it out. Do you think He is pronouncing judgment on any country/city/town/people today? Why/why not?

4. It is clear in this chapter, and this book, that God hates sin and is a God of vengeance. Does this fit with your own picture of God?

5. If God hates sin, and is a God of vengeance, then why does He not judge those who are killing and torturing others today?

6. Why does Nahum compare Nineveh to a prostitute? In some translations 1:4 speaks about 'the multitude of the whoredoms of the well-favoured harlot'. Why do you think Nahum uses such an illustration when speaking against Nineveh?

7. What do you think are the answers to the two questions that are asked in 3:7

8. What might be the purpose of referring in 3:8 to 'Thebes' (or No Amon in some translations)?

9. Can you identify with those in 3:19 who 'clap their hands' at the news of the downfall of Nineveh? Have you ever had similar feelings when you see justice prevail?

10. What is the most significant lesson you have learned from studying this book of Nahum?

Don't forget to pray

Ask the Holy Spirit to give you a right understanding of the character of God. Ask God to give you the desire to read and understand His word, so you are able to learn more about who He really is. Pray that the Lord will reveal Himself to you so that you know the God of the Bible, and not a god of your own imagination.

Nahum Chapter 3 – Notes

We read in this chapter about killings, piles of corpses, witchcraft and other things. Nineveh is called a city of blood. Today we hear of similar things happening in other countries i.e. people being beheaded, tortured and killed with unimaginable violence.

Our God has not changed and His wrath and anger against such injustice and sin is the same today as it was in the time of Nineveh. Just because we do not see judgment carried out against terrorists and murderers, does not mean that God will not judge. We know He is patient, but He is also just.

He has pronounced judgment against the evil in the world in His Word, and what God says He will do, He does. So we can be sure that He will judge. But this will be in His time, and according to His plan and purpose for this world.

It seems that Nineveh thought that God would not act, or did not see, all that was happening. They did not listen to the prophet Nahum and, as we know from history, judgment did come soon afterwards. Probably many people feel the same way today. As God is not acting now, they assume He will not, or that He doesn't see, or even that He does not exist. When the Day of Judgment comes, each person will finally understand that God does exist and that He hates sin.

We need to ensure that as Christians we do not try and paint a picture of God which is not true to the Bible. Some of us emphasise one aspect of the character of God and overlook, or minimise others. Our God is love, and contained in that love is His justice, His holiness, His wrath against evil, His righteousness, His vengeance and much more as well.

Also, within that love is God's amazing patience. Without that patience humankind would no longer exist! And because of that patience God is still waiting for many more to repent and turn to Him so that they do not have to face judgment.

Nineveh is guilty of spiritual adultery. She has turned away from the living God to chase after other gods. She has turned away from all that is good, and is pursuing evil. This is no doubt why she is likened to a prostitute. She seduced neighbouring nations and encouraged them into idolatry. Nineveh wanted to be the metropolis of the world and to have everyone subject to her. She did not just use war but also used wealth, power and greatness to achieve this. She wanted the first place. She wanted to be a universal monarchy. And for this, and for her tyranny, God has a quarrel with her. He must always have the first place, and He hated, and still hates, to see the shedding of blood, robbery, witchcraft, and man's inhumanity to man. Eventually God does judge.

The Ninevites had behaved so deplorably that when judgment fell on them there would be no-one to comfort them and no-one to mourn for them. Those that show no pity towards others, will have no pity shown them on the day of judgment. I will make you a spectacle, or an example, God says through the prophet. This is a salient lesson for us today. We look with horror at many things that are done today, and the proud way in which these are often carried out. But this prophecy makes it clear that the greater the pride and the show, the greater the shame and destruction. Proverbs 11:2 reminds us that when we are proud, we are heading for a fall. 'When pride cometh then cometh shame: but with the lowly is wisdom.' Proverbs 11:2 KJV. 'When pride comes, then comes disgrace, but with humility comes wisdom.' Proverbs 11:2 NIV.

When the prophet refers to Thebes, Bible scholars believe this refers to the destruction of a city which would have been well-known in Nineveh, and still fresh in their memory. Nahum was reminding the Ninevites that if destruction had come on that city, then likewise it could, and would, fall on them too.

We all like to see justice and probably do rejoice when we see those who commit evil being punished. Nevertheless today we can still tell people the good news about Jesus because we know that God is always willing to forgive if anyone repents and turns away from evil. At the same time we must remember that we have an urgent message, because one day that good news will no longer be available. God is patient, but He will not allow evil to continue forever.

Habakkuk
Background and Introduction

The name Habakkuk means to embrace or wrestle. We see the prophet wrestling with God in this book which documents a number of conversations between him and God. In these talks we are given some insight into the way God uses the wicked to achieve His purposes and the issue of ultimate justice.

Habakkuk probably prophesied some time between 620-600BC and about 20 years later his prophecy was fulfilled. He represents the final voice to Judah before she was destroyed and carried off into captivity by the Babylonians. He was probably a contemporary of Jeremiah who lived to experience the things Habakkuk foretold.

This book grapples with the problem which has arisen in the minds of men throughout the ages. Why do the wicked prosper and the righteous suffer?

The prophet complains to God that justice is not seen among his own people. He complains about the suffering of many good people. But when God tells him the way in which he will bring justice, he complains about that too!

The book of Habakkuk is very relevant today. He really cared about the state of Israel. He is perhaps like someone today who is so filled with the Holy Spirit that he is grieving about the violence and injustice that he sees and is pleading with God to do something about it.

But as Habakkuk found out, God does not always (or often?) answer our prayers in the way we expect. It is sometimes not easy to accept the answer He does give.

But through it all Habakkuk continues to pour out his heart to God. The book begins with complaints, fear, worries and anxiety, and ends with a beautiful section of praise to God. The last few verses of this book are some of the most well-known in the Bible – but sometimes we forget what Habakkuk had to go through before he reached this point. He had wrestled with God and been brought to absolute trust and surrender. He had found peace in his heart and soul irrespective of the circumstances around him.

What a great transformation we will see in Habakkuk as we study this book. In the space of three small chapters he is changed from someone full of complaints and anxiety to someone who is worshipping God in full trust and surrender.

Study 4 – Chapter 1 (Habakkuk)
Habakkuk complains to God

Discuss/think about

How do you feel when you see evil men prospering? And how do you feel when you see good people suffering as a result? What do you think God should do about this?

Read Habakkuk chapter 1

1. With some prophets we are introduced to them in the first few verses of the book and some detail is given about their lives. What do you think the reason could be for saying nothing about Habakkuk and his background at the beginning of this book?

2. Do you ever feel like Habakkuk? Why/why not?

3. It is clear that Habakkuk felt a real passion about these matters of violence and injustice. How passionate do you feel about injustice in the world today?

4. How does God answer Habakkuk?

5. Why do you think God says in 1:5 that He was going to do something which 'you would not believe even if you were told'?

6. Why is Habakkuk not happy with God's answer?

7. Can you think of an example in your own life where you have complained to God about something and His answer has been totally unexpected?

8. What do you think is the answer to Habakkuk's questions in 1:13?

9. What aspects of Habakkuk's character can we see in this chapter?

10. What can we learn about God's character in this chapter?

Don't forget to pray

Ask God to help you become passionate about injustice in the world, so that you speak to Him about it and do what you can, when you can, to promote justice.

Habakkuk Chapter 1 – Notes

Most of us are very unhappy to see evil prosper and good people suffer. Whether we feel as passionately as Habakkuk about it though, is a question we do well to ask ourselves. We sometimes complain to God perhaps about things that affect us personally. But do we feel like this for our nation? For the state of the church? For our world? Habakkuk really cared about Israel. Do we really care about the state of the world today? And if we do, how often do we pray to God about it? And are we prepared to help in any way?

It is easy sometimes to expect God to act, but at the same time not be prepared for Him to work through us! C.B Samuel is a theologian and Bible teacher and has been involved with much relief and development work in India. He says this, 'a prayer in which we are not open to being part of the solution will never be answered.' This may explain why some of our prayers are not answered!

We know very little about this prophet. We are not told of his background or his genealogy. Perhaps this is because he could represent anyone of us regarding our conversations with God.

God answered Habakkuk in a totally unexpected way by telling him He was going to use the Babylonians to destroy Judah. Habakkuk is clearly taken by surprise because he complains again. Surely you won't do this? Surely you won't allow these wicked men to do these terrible things to your people?

This is perhaps why God says that His solution will be difficult to believe. It is hard for us to understand the way in which God is able to use wicked men to accomplish His plans and purposes. However, this should also give us great faith and confidence in God because He is in control of everything and He is working everything out in His time and in His own way.

Thus the answer to Habakkuk's questions in verse 13 is that God is in control and His ways are not our ways. He is also patient – 2 Peter 3:9. So although He does not judge as quickly as we would like Him to sometimes, He does judge! And when His judgment comes it is sure and certain. We will see when we study Zephaniah that he speaks of the great Day of the Lord. There is a time coming when all evil will be judged absolutely and forever.

So the Lord tells Habakkuk that although He is going to use the Babylonians to destroy Judah, yet the Babylonians will be judged because of their wickedness. God is able to use those who are opposed to Him to work out His plans and purposes, but they will still be judged for their wicked behaviour.

Habakkuk seems to be a man of passion and integrity. He has a great love of justice and righteousness. He is also persistent and grapples with God about these great questions of evil and suffering. We would do well to follow his example.

We see many characteristics of God in this chapter but the main ones are His anger and wrath against evil, and His ability and desire for justice.

Study 5 – Chapter 2 (Habakkuk)
The Lord's answer

Discuss/think about

When you pray, do you pray with the expectation that God will answer you? What do you do if it appears that He is saying nothing? Have you had any experiences you can share of praying for something for a long time, and then God finally answering you in a totally unexpected way?

Read Habakkuk chapter 2

1. Contrast and compare Habakkuk's attitude in 1:2 and 2:1. Can you see any change in his attitude?

2. The prophet says at the beginning of chapter two, 'I will *stand* at my watch, I will *station* myself on the ramparts'. How might this help us to understand how we can become more adept at hearing God speak to us?

3. What experience have you had of God speaking to you? How/when has He done this?

4. Why was Habakkuk told by God to write down (2:2) what He was saying?

5. What do you think God means in verse 3 (2:3) when He says that the vision, or revelation, waits for an appointed time?

6. Why does God wait for 'an appointed time'? Why doesn't He just act straight away?

7. Look at Romans 1:17; Galatians 3:11 and Hebrews 10:38. What is meant by 'the righteous will live by his faith' (2:4)? Why was this relevant for the time when Habakkuk was alive? Why is it relevant for us today?

8. What sins are mentioned in 2:5?   Are these still relevant today?

9. What is God's view of these sins?   How does He react?   Is His view or His reaction any different today?

10. What encouragement can we find in this chapter which might help us today?

Don't forget to pray

Look at Habakkuk 2:20; Zechariah 2:13 and Psalm 46:10.   Take some time out to 'be still' before God and ask Him to speak to you about something which you have on your heart.

Habakkuk Chapter 2 – Notes

Chapter one begins with Habakkuk pouring out his heart to God and complaining that God is not listening. But when we come to chapter two his attitude is different. Now he is expecting God to answer and prepared to wait until He does so. We can also have a similar experience. As we pour out our hearts to God, and develop a relationship with Him, so we will find that He does answer. And as we experience this, so we learn to wait patiently in trust and faith.

Habakkuk stands watching and stations himself before God as he waits for the answer. There are several verses in the Bible which speak about 'being still' before God e.g. Zechariah 2:13 and Psalm 46:10. It is often when we intentionally come before God, and shut out all other distractions, that He speaks directly into our hearts. Jesus tells us that we should go into our room and shut the door – Matthew 6:6. This could mean actually shutting the door to avoid being disturbed. It could also mean shutting the door of our minds to all other distractions. We should learn to cultivate the presence of God in this way, if we want to hear Him speak.

Habakkuk was told to write down the vision. Then when it came true, there was an accurate record of his prophecy. It is also a wonderful legacy for us in the Bible. We can learn so much from Habakkuk. Things that are written down can be preserved and passed on from one generation to another. It is also a useful discipline to write down what we believe God may be saying to us. It is a wonderful way to strengthen our faith because we can look back and see how faithful God has been in our lives. If nothing is written down, it is so easy to forget!

There is an appointed time for everything that God does. In this case the judgment which was coming was deferred but certain. Likewise today, the judgment of evil in this world is deferred, but certain. There will be a Day of Judgment. This would be another reason why the prophet had to write down the vision, so that it could be reviewed afterwards and the events compared with it. It is also a warning. God often warns before He acts, and if such warnings are written down then those who choose to ignore Him have no excuse.

We need to learn to wait for God's time. 'Though it linger, wait for it.' The promise may seem silent. It may seem to us that God does not hear. But there will always be an answer and it will come at the appointed time. 2 Peter 3:9 reminds us that God is patient and does not want anyone to perish. And so He warns and waits. But eventually He acts.

We so often fail to understand that God is working many things out at the same time. What seems to us as unnecessary delay, is the working out of God's perfect plan and purpose for each of us and for our world. Isaiah tells us (Isaiah 55:8-9) that the Lord says, "For my thoughts are not your thoughts, neither are your ways my ways," declares the Lord. "As the heavens are higher than the earth, so are my ways higher than your ways and my thoughts than your thoughts."

Habakkuk was reminded that righteousness in God's eyes, depends on our believing Him. Abraham was reckoned to be righteous, because He believed God. Likewise today, we can be declared righteous if we believe God. If we believe in His plan of salvation. If we believe on the Lord Jesus Christ then we will be saved and declared righteous by God – Acts 16:31 and Romans 10:9.

The sins listed in this verse 2:5 can be covered by 'the lust of the flesh, the lust of the eyes, and the pride of life' (1 John 2:16). These are just as prevalent today and God's anger against them remains the same. Such sin will always be judged. If we confess our sin and repent, then the judgment for that sin has been borne by Jesus on the cross. But if we do not accept what Jesus has done on our behalf, then we will have to face the judgment ourselves. We read in chapter one that 'your eyes are too pure to look at evil'. God will not tolerate evil and it will eventually be completely judged and banished forever.

Thus we can be encouraged by reading Habakkuk. God does not ignore the evil in the world today. He sees everything that is going on and one day He will judge. However, in the meantime the good news about Jesus is still being proclaimed. God is patiently waiting for more people to be saved. He knows when that will be. He knows exactly the right time to act. He always has done, still does, and always will do exactly the right thing, at exactly the right time. We can be encouraged to see this in Habakkuk and know that we serve the same God. He never changes.

Study 6 – Chapter 3 (Habakkuk)
Habakkuk's prayer

Discuss/think about

How do you/would you feel if you are going through a severe trial, and someone suggests you should praise God? Is it easy or difficult to praise God when things seem to be going wrong in our lives? Why?

Read Habakkuk chapter 3

1. Compare the first verse of chapter two with the first few verses of chapter three. Do you see any change in the prophet's attitude towards God? If so, why do you think this may have occurred?

2. Chapter three opens by telling us this is a prayer of Habakkuk *on shigionoth*. What does this mean? Does this passage we have read remind you of any other parts of the Bible?

3. This chapter is called a 'prayer'. Is the prophet asking for anything?

4. Why does the prophet look back over the years and remind God of what He has done before?

5. Can you think of some of the things that God has done for the Israelites in the past that Habakkuk may be referring to in verses 3:3-3:7? (You may want to check out Exodus 19:16-20; Deuteronomy 33:2; Deuteronomy 32:8-9; Judges 3:8; and Judges 7:13.)

6. Why does Habakkuk react so strongly in 3:16? Have you ever felt like this in the presence of God?

7. Although he obviously feels afraid, he is prepared to wait patiently for the calamity. How is he able to do this?

8. The prophet looks ahead in 3:17 to a day that he believes is coming soon – when there will be famine and disaster. He supposes himself to be deprived of everything but He is still able to rejoice in the Lord. How is this possible?

9. Are you able to rejoice in the Lord even when things are going wrong in your life? If you are studying this book in a group, are you willing to share any experience you have had of being able to be joyful, even though your circumstances have not been good?

10. What happens if we praise God in the middle of our trials? What was the result for Habakkuk when he praised God, even though he was dreading what was about to happen?

Don't forget to pray

Try to find time each day to praise God, irrespective of your circumstances, and see what happens!

Habakkuk Chapter 3 – Notes

Habakkuk had a real experience with God. First he spoke with God and poured out his heart. Then God answered him. Habakkuk then continues his conversation with God and asks many questions, but this time he knows that God is going to answer him. He stands and waits expectantly for God to answer. Then the Lord does answer and tells Habakkuk some of the things that are going to happen. The prayer in chapter three is a result of these exchanges with God, and the prophet begins to intercede on behalf of Israel.

If we have conversations with God then it will change us. If we understand what is going to happen in the future, it will have an effect on us. We will want to intercede on behalf of our world, the church, and those who do not know Jesus as their Saviour. We can learn so much from Habakkuk and each of us can be like him in some way. We can all learn to pour out our hearts to God, and to intercede on behalf of others asking that in His wrath, God will remember to be merciful.

'Shigionoth' is probably a musical term and we can see many similarities between this chapter and some of the Psalms. The Amplified version of the Bible translates the introduction to chapter three of Habakkuk as follows: 'A prayer of Habakkuk the prophet, set to wild, enthusiastic, and triumphal music.' We can see therefore that Habakkuk is worshipping and praising God, even though he knew terrible times were coming.

The prophet is asking God to be merciful. He is interceding on behalf of Israel, reminding God of all the wonderful things He has done before for His people, and pleading with Him to be merciful. We too can remind God (and ourselves) of all He has done in the past, and ask Him to act in a similar way again. When we pray for revival we can remind God of what He has done in many places in the past, and ask Him to do this again. We can intercede on behalf of the church too. Although she has committed many sins, we can still ask for mercy because we know God is merciful.

The prophets often interceded with God on behalf of the people, when God had revealed what He intended to do. We too can intercede on behalf of others, because we know that God will punish evil, but also that He is just and merciful. We cannot really understand the full effect of our prayers, but we do know that God hears and answers prayer.

Habakkuk may have been referring to some of the following, as He reminds God of things He has done in the past. The Lord descending on Mount Sinai (Exodus 19:16-20 and Deuteronomy 33:2); the division of the inheritance to the different tribes of Israel (Deuteronomy 32:8-9); the Lord was angry with Israel and sold them into the hands of Cushan-Rishathaim (Judges 3:8) and Gideon's dream when the loaf of barley bread struck the Midianite camp (Judges 7:13). You may be able to think of several other incidents that Habakkuk refers to in this chapter.

Habakkuk was deeply affected by hearing from God. If we hear God speak to us it will also affect us in some way, even if not so drastically as Habakkuk. Moses face shone when he had been speaking with God. What effect do your prayers have on you? Do you hear from God? What is your experience of this?

Habakkuk seems to have complete trust in God. Even though he is afraid, he does not lose his trust in God. He does not turn away from God. He is prepared to wait patiently, trusting God, for all that is to come in the future. He is perhaps able to do this because he knows God. He has a real personal relationship with God, he knows some of the characteristics of God, and therefore is prepared to trust Him. He can look back on the way in which God has acted in the past and remind himself that his God is merciful and good. Therefore, in spite of what may happen, he knows that God will do what is right.

God is always worthy of our praise because of who He is. We can remind ourselves of His wonderful love which has been demonstrated in the death of Jesus on the cross. Paul tells us in Romans 8:32 that, 'He who did not spare his own Son, but gave him up for us all—how will he not also, along with him, graciously give us all things?' Therefore, even though we sometimes do not understand what is happening in our own lives, and in the lives of others, we can still praise God.

And then as we start to praise God in the middle of our trials, we often find that He lifts our spirits, strengthens our faith, and we experience an overwhelming sense of His great love. So, even though it is sometimes hard to praise God when we are feeling low, nevertheless if we start to do this, we find that God turns it into a great blessing for us!

Zephaniah
Background and Introduction

The recurring themes in the Minor Prophets are judgment, repentance and restoration/salvation. Zephaniah covers all three themes in his short prophecy.

His name means 'protected by the Lord' and he probably wrote this book sometime between 635-610BC. He was a prophet to Judah during the reign of Josiah. Zephaniah condemns the very sins that Josiah lamented. Josiah was the last of Judah's righteous rulers and when the 'book of the law' was found, he lamented and repented of the many sins of his people. You can find more information about Josiah in 2 Chronicles 34 and 35. When he was only 20 years old, Josiah began a programme of national reform. His repentance resulted in action!

However, Zephaniah was still called by God during Josiah's reign to prophesy judgments for Jerusalem which began to fall within the next 50 years.

There is probably no book in the Bible, other than Revelation, which speaks so clearly of the great 'Day of the Lord'. The prophecy is therefore extremely relevant for us today. The 'Day of the Lord' or 'Judgment Day' refers to the punishment which was coming, and did come, for Jerusalem because the people refused to repent and listen to God. The same prophecies could also refer to judgment at the end of this period of time in which we now live. Zephaniah speaks of the Day of the Lord which will come with fury and force, and he also speaks about the aftermath of that day.

The prophet speaks about a time of grief and pain for those who have rejected God, but a time of blessing and praise for those who love Him.

God is perfectly just and perfectly righteous in all He does. He warns and then He acts. The book of Zephaniah is divided into three sections. First, the warning of judgment which is coming – chapter one. Then a call to repentance in chapter two, followed by the punishment which follows because the people did not listen. Then finally from 3:9-3:20 we read of salvation and the new day for God's people. Judgment, punishment (because there was no repentance) and restoration/salvation for those who love God.

Study 7 – Chapter 1 (Zephaniah)
Warning of judgment

Discuss/think about

How often do you think about the 'Day of the Lord' or 'Judgment Day'? If you thought about this more often do you think it would affect how you live now? Why/why not?

Read Zephaniah chapter 1

1. We know that Zephaniah prophesied during the reign of Josiah but we are not told exactly when. After reading this chapter do you think he prophesied at the beginning, middle, or end of Josiah's reign? Discuss your reasons.

2. How do you feel when you read of the coming destruction in verses 1:2-3? Many Bible scholars believe this warning also applies to our world today. How do you feel about that?

3. How do these verses fit in with our knowledge of a God of love?

4. Why do you think the people were worshipping God and also Molech (1:5)? What relevance/warning does this have for us today?

5. Why are the 'princes and the king's sons' especially selected for punishment (1:8)?

6. We read in 1:12 that there are those who think 'the Lord will do nothing, either good or bad.' Are you one of those who think like this? Why/why not? Do you know people who think like this? Do you pray for them?

7. Do you believe that the great day of the Lord is near and coming quickly (1:14)? Read Matthew 24:26-35 and compare this with Zephaniah 1:14-18.

8. Read Ezekiel 7:19; Proverbs 11:4; and Ecclesiastes 5:10 and 5:13. Compare these verses with Zephaniah 1:18. What does this tell us about wealth and money?

9. How can we be encouraged even when we read about this terrible time?

10. Having read and studied this chapter, will it make a difference to the way you live and interact with others who do not know God?

Don't forget to pray

Ask the Holy Spirit to give you an urgency which compels you to speak to others about Jesus, before the Great Day of the Lord arrives.

Zephaniah Chapter 1 – Notes

Zephaniah tells us at the beginning of this book that he prophesied during the reign of Josiah but he does not tell us the exact time. So although we know he probably prophesied between 635BC and 610BC we don't know exactly when. Bible scholars have different views. Some believe it must have been at the beginning of Josiah's reign, and as a result Josiah and the people repented. This would seem to be supported by the fact that Josiah lamented that they were not following the 'book of the law' (2 Chronicles 34) and then initiated a programme of reform. However, other scholars believe the prophecy came towards the end of Josiah's reign when the people were turning away from God once more. In any case, it seems that the people were only temporarily pious, influenced no doubt by Josiah. But it is clear that both before and after Josiah's reign the Israelites turned their back on God, and chased after other gods.

The warnings in this chapter could equally well apply to our world today. Many people have turned away from God – even in the so-called Christian western world. However, the good news about Jesus is still being spread, so we can continue to pray that many more people will repent and turn to Christ before the Day of Judgment.

Sometimes the question is asked, 'how could a God of love send people to hell?' But the real question should be, 'how could a God of love not send people to hell, if they persist in evil and do not want to accept His love?' Each one of us has a choice, and each person in hell will have chosen to be there. God does not want any person to perish, but each of us is given free choice. We can choose good or evil, heaven or hell, God's love or our own way.

It seems that the Israelites had decided to hedge their bets and worship both God and Moloch! They knew all about the God of Israel, of course, because this was the religion of their country. It had been for as long as they could remember and was passed down through the generations. So perhaps they thought it would be best not to quit it completely, but instead try to improve on it by joining it with the worship of Moloch! They had no visible representation of God, and therefore wanted an image. What better than the image of Moloch – a king?

But it is a solemn warning to us, as well as them, that those who think they can divide their affection and worship between God and idols, i.e. something or someone else, will find how fierce God's wrath can be. He will not have only part of our lives and worship, He desires it all. And there can be no mixing or fellowship between light and darkness, Christ and the devil.

The princes and those in authority are especially responsible, because they lead others astray. In this case they were perhaps especially proud because of all their riches. Jesus tells us in Luke 12:48, 'From everyone who has been given much, much will be demanded; and from the one who has been entrusted with much, much more will be asked.'

As time goes on it is easy to think that perhaps God does not see, or does not care, about the evil in the world. We do hear people say today, that they don't believe in God. Often the reason they give is that they see nothing being done about the suffering in the world. However, Peter tells us in 2 Peter 3:9, 'The Lord is not slow in keeping his promise, as some understand slowness. Instead he is patient with you, not wanting anyone to perish, but everyone to come to repentance.' It is fascinating to compare some of the things that Jesus said about His coming, with this passage in Zephaniah about the Day of the Lord. Matthew 24:26-35 is one such example.

When we compare Zephaniah 1:18 with Ezekiel 7:19; Proverbs 11:4; and Ecclesiastes 5:10 and 5:13, we can see each Scripture tells the same story. And throughout the Bible we are told not to desire riches, and not to trust in them if we have them. Money can be a terrible temptation and Timothy tells us in 1 Timothy 6:10 that, 'For the love of money is a root of all kinds of evil. Some people, eager for money, have wandered from the faith and pierced themselves with many griefs.' Why are we so reluctant to learn this lesson?!

We can be encouraged even when reading such a chapter as this. We know a God of love who is working out all His plans and purposes for each of us as individuals, and for our world. We can trust in that love and know that He will do everything in a just, righteous and perfect way. No-one will be able to say that what God does at the end of time, is not fair. Abraham says to God in Genesis 18, ' Far be it from you to do such a thing—to kill the righteous with the wicked, treating the righteous and the wicked alike. Far be it from you! Will not the Judge of all the earth do right?' And we can echo Abraham's trust in God and say with him, 'will not the Judge of all the earth do right?' Yes of course He will.

'What, then, shall we say in response to these things? If God is for us, who can be against us? He who did not spare his own Son, but gave him up for us all—how will he not also, along with him, graciously give us all things? Who will bring any charge against those whom God has chosen? It is God who justifies. Who then is the one who condemns? No one. Christ Jesus who died—more than that, who was raised to life—is at the right hand of God and is also interceding for us.' Romans 8:31-34.

Study 8 – Chapter 2 (Zephaniah)
Punishment

Discuss/think about

What does it mean to be 'repentant'? When/how do you repent? Is it possible today for a nation to repent?

Read Zephaniah chapter 2

1. Why do you think the nation is told to 'gather together' (2:1)?

2. What is the tone of the first three verses of this chapter (2:1-3)?

3. What is God saying to the people in these first three verses, and why is He saying this?

4. How do these verses apply to us today?

5. Who/what were Philistia, Moab, Ammon, Cush and Assyria?

6. Why were these nations being punished?

7. What do we learn about God in this chapter?

8. Is God still the same today? What warnings do you think He may be giving today?

9. What do you think would be the result today, if a prophet spoke like this against our own country?

10. What do you think would be God's response if we, as a nation, humbled ourselves and repented?

Don't forget to pray

Pray for your own nation/country, that it will turn to God in repentance and God's wrath will be turned away as a result. Pray for all those you know who do not know Jesus. Pray that they will repent and turn to God before it is too late.

Zephaniah Chapter 2 – Notes

The word repentance is often used to mean 'saying sorry'. But it goes far beyond speech or even feelings. The true meaning of repentance in the Bible includes a change. A change of mind, a change of heart, a change of both mental and spiritual attitude towards sin. True repentance would involve action, as well as words.

The call to gather together is a warning and an exhortation. Gather together all you who know the only true God, and who are willing to repent. All those who do this, and who repent, will be saved from the wrath of God. This message was true then when Zephaniah prophesied, and it is still true today. God does not want anyone to perish. But if we refuse His offer of grace, mercy and salvation, then He has no option. So He calls out to the Israelites through Zephaniah, humble yourselves and I will keep you safe in the day of my wrath.

God's message throughout the Bible is so clear. I wonder why we so often miss it! My way, not your way. Repent and humble yourselves and all will be well!

And so the Israelites are told to gather themselves together, and to seek the Lord, before the decree of judgment actually happens and His fierce anger overcomes them. God always distinguishes between the righteous and the unrighteous, those who recognise Him, and those who do not.

The first three verses of this chapter represent a warning and a plea - just as the Gospel message today also represents a warning and a plea. Repent and be saved. Refuse and be judged.

Philistia, Moab, Ammon, Cush and Assyria were all enemies of Israel. The judgment would fall on the whole territory of Israel, which was occupied in many parts by strangers who were hostile to the Israelites. The effect of this would be to leave the whole land free for the possession of Israel, and eventually God would bring those who had not forsaken Him, to possess it. The Lord would judge all the gods of the earth, and men would worship only Him.

So the nations, who had been used to punish Israel, would now themselves be punished. God's ways are not our ways! He is able to work through evil men, to accomplish all His plans.

So here just in this one chapter we see a God who wants people to repent, but is also prepared to judge evil in a very drastic way. We know a God of love and that love includes righteousness, justice, anger, wrath, hatred of sin and much more besides.

The recurring characters in the Minor Prophets (which include Zephaniah) are – the Lord, His people (Israel and Judah) and the Gentile nations. The recurring themes are – judgment, repentance and restoration.

We must remember that we know a God whose character never changes. He is, was and always will be the same. Therefore, we can learn much from Zephaniah about our God. The warnings of judgment are just as relevant today as they were then. God's love is just the same as it was then. Repent and be saved. Refuse and be judged.

Study 9 – Chapter 3 (Zephaniah)
A New Day for God's people

Discuss/think about

What is the purpose of judgment and justice in our world? What is the purpose of God's judgment?

Read Zephaniah chapter 3

1. How do you think God feels about Jerusalem in these verses 3:1-5?

2. Why is it particularly sad and displeasing to God that Jerusalem, of all places, should behave in such a wicked way?

3. Read Deuteronomy 23:14 and Leviticus 20:26. What is the relevance of these verses to the people of Jerusalem to whom Zephaniah is speaking?

4. Read Ezekiel 23:9-11. We know that Oholibah represents Jerusalem (Ezekiel 23:4). God punished the wickedness of the Assyrians (Oholah) and yet still Jerusalem did not learn from this. How does this compare with Zephaniah 3:6-8?

5. What does God want to achieve through this punishment which is promised for Jerusalem?

6. What does it mean to 'call on the name of the Lord' (3:9)?

7. How would you summarize these three different sections of chapter three – i.e 3:1-8; 3:9-13 and 3:14-20?

8. Look at John 1:49. How can we link what we know about Jesus, to what we have read here in Zephaniah?

9. How and why can the section 3:14-20 apply to us today?

10. What personal experience have you had of verse 17 (3:17)?

Don't forget to pray

Matt Redman wrote his song 'the Father's love' from his experience of Zephaniah 3:17. Take some time out to listen to this song and praise God for His wonderful love to you personally.

Zephaniah chapter 3 – Notes

The purpose of judgment in our world is to administer justice. Written over the entrance to the law courts in New York is this. 'The true administration of justice is the firmest pillar of good government.' Judgments that are passed should always be to protect the innocent and punish evil. If judgment is fair and just then it should be a warning to others not to sin in the same way. It can also mean the guilty one realises how wrong he/she has been, and lives a changed life. However, we know that often judgment is not fair and therefore has the opposite effect. People think they can get away with doing wrong, and are encouraged to continue. Innocent people continue to suffer because of a lack of justice in our world.

Those who read the Bible see God's judgments from Genesis to Revelation. If we fail to see God's purpose for judgment, we will view it negatively and think of it as punishment instead of grace and mercy. However, if we understand God's purpose for judgment, we will see why it is needed, and recognize that it is a wonderful work of grace, and that many blessings flow from it!

From Zephaniah we can see that God will always punish the guilty. However, we also see that He is slow to anger and always gives warnings and opportunities to change. Why is He slow to anger? Because God is waiting to see if a person will repent! It is repentance that God desires. He only resorts to judgment when repentance is resisted and refused. As we turn from our sin and toward the Lord's grace and mercy we are spared the judgments that would have come upon us.

This is true both for individuals as well as nations. If a nation has been prophesied against as we see here in Zephaniah —that is, God has stated that He will send forth judgments upon it—and then that nation repents, it is spared from God's wrath. We saw in 2:1-3 that there was an opportunity to repent. And God will always be slow to anger, giving both individuals and nations time to repent. But if that repentance does not come about, then we can expect that the judgment will come, just as the Lord has said through Zephaniah, through many other prophets, and through His Word.

It was especially sad that Jerusalem behaved in this way. The people there had so many advantages. They knew God's law, they knew how much He had blessed them in the past, they knew they were special in His eyes. They knew God's presence among them, and all the advantages that could come from knowing and obeying Him, and yet they persisted in their disobedience.

They also knew God's requirement that they should be different. That they should be 'holy' and represent Him. Deuteronomy 23:14 and Leviticus 20:26 are just two of many examples where God's requirements are clear.

Time and again we see God speaking through the prophets, and acting in judgment against Israel's enemies. Surely Jerusalem would see, and learn, from this? But just as Ezekiel prophesies (Ezekiel 23:9-11) she is like an adulterous sister. Rather than acting differently to the nations, she copies what they do – and in fact, is even worse!

This should be a warning to us who are part of the Church. We are called to be holy and different from those who do not know Christ. If we think that God's judgment will not apply to us just because we 'go to church' we could not be more wrong.

But God's judgments always have blessing in mind. We see the wonderful result of His judgment in 3:14-20. In the same way, God has great blessing in mind for all eternity for those who want it. But first there has to be judgment, so that all evil is banished forever.

There is a call to prayer for the Israelites, and for us, in 3:9. To call on the name of the Lord means to communicate with God – i.e. to pray. To trust that He is good and will save us. To believe God and accept His offer of salvation. Thus Paul tells us in Romans 10:13 that, 'everyone who calls on the name of the Lord, will be saved.'

This chapter three of Zephaniah is really divided into three sections. The first section is a description of the judgment and punishment which is coming for Jerusalem. The second section shows us what

God intends to achieve by this work of judgment. The third section is a song of praise from those who have been delivered.

In John 1:49, Nathaniel realised who Jesus was. He knew He was the King of Israel. He realised that Zephaniah 3:15 was talking about this very person who was standing in front of Him. Do we also understand this?

If we have accepted God's plan of salvation, and accepted Jesus as our Lord and Saviour, then we can join in the song of praise in 3:14-20. Just as Zephaniah preached judgment, repentance and restoration for Jerusalem, so the Gospel message is preached today. The Lord is coming soon, judgment is near, repent and believe, and you will be safe and saved for all eternity.

The experience of being in God's presence, and having a direct and personal experience of His love, is available to every one of us.

Study 10 – Conclusions
What is God saying to us?

Discuss/think about

Do you believe that the messages of the Minor Prophets, and especially Nahum, Habakkuk and Zephaniah are relevant to us today? How and why?

1. Summarize the key message from Nahum.

2. Summarize the key message from Habakkuk.

3. Summarize the key message from Zephaniah.

4. Compare and contrast these messages. Are they all the same or different in some way?

5. What is the key learning point for you from having studied these three books?

6. What have you personally learned about God from studying these books?

7. What can we learn as a church from the warnings in these books?

8. Do you feel that you personally need to take any action as a result of reading Nahum, Habakkuk and Zephaniah?

9. Will these three prophets help you in the way you pray in future?

10. Spend some time meditating on Nahum 1:7; Habakkuk 3:17-19 and Zephaniah 3:17.

Don't forget to pray

Ask God to help you apply all you have learned from studying these three Minor Prophets. Ask Him to teach you to read the Old Testament prophets, not as history lessons but as guidance for you today. Pray that you will learn more about our awesome God as a result.

Study 10 – Notes

We have seen that the messages from Nahum, Habakkuk and Zephaniah are very relevant to us today. Just as God was in a special relationship with Israel during the time of these prophets, so He is in a special relationship with the Church today. And each one of us, who are part of His Church, can also have a special and personal relationship with God. The Church, of course, is not one particular denomination or group. The Church consists of every person who knows and loves the Lord Jesus Christ. Every person who has come under the shelter of the blood of Jesus which was poured out on the cross for each one of us.

The key message from Nahum could be that God will judge the unrighteous and vindicate the righteous. The message of Habakkuk could be that any nation or person that trusts in itself, or himself, rather than God will fall. We can see in each of these three books how much God hates pride. And Zephaniah preaches the message that Judgment is coming. There is no doubt about this, and it should be a challenge to each of us – where will you stand when it comes?

The messages are different, but also the same. They tell of a God who hates evil and who will eventually judge it completely. But they also tell of a God who loves each of us and is not willing that anyone should perish. Peter tells us in 2 Peter 3:9 that, 'The Lord is not slow in keeping his promise, as some understand slowness. Instead he is patient with you, not wanting anyone to perish, but everyone to come to repentance.'

We should be able to learn much personally, and as a church, from reading these books. Perhaps it should increase our desire to live here in a way that pleases God. Perhaps it will help us to speak to others more urgently about their need of a Saviour. Perhaps it will increase our horror of sin, so we repent more quickly when we fail. Maybe as a church we need to gather and repent of our lukewarm attitude at times to the One who has called us, and ask Him what He wants us to do. And maybe we could pray for our nation – that God will be merciful and cause repentance so that we are not judged for the many ways in which we have turned our back on Him.

And finally, we can be greatly encouraged by meditating on these wonderful verses in Nahum 1:7; Habakkuk 3:17-19 and Zephaniah 3:17. What an awesome God we know!

Other Books by Margaret Weston

Margaret Weston is the author of the BSBP series and the 'How do I know?' series.

'How do I know?' Series

The 'How do I know?' series consists of an ongoing conversation between two people. The first book **'How do I know I know God?'** would be invaluable for you if you claim to be a Christian but are not sure whether you do have a personal relationship with God. It would also be helpful for those who have no faith and yet are intrigued by those who do. It is a best-seller in Christian Evangelism.

One of the reviews on Amazon.com says this about the book. "Every question you've ever had about God is considered in the light of what the Bible says. If you count yourself as a skeptic, I think you'll find every argument you've ever had with God will be resolved in this book."

'How do I know what God wants me to do?' is the second book in the series and is written as a challenge to the author herself and to Christians world-wide. Will you realise your potential in Christ? Will you take action - or if you are already doing so, will you continue to take action - to advance God's kingdom in our generation?

The third book in the series is **'How do I know God answers prayer?'** which is a question every Christian should be able to answer! However, the book also looks at the subject of prayer in a wider sense as the two unknown people continue to discuss this subject together. You will find questions that are often asked by those who know God and also those who do not.

BSBP Series

This series is intended to be for a specific group of people – those who really want to study the Bible but find they simply do not have the time. Life can be so hectic and whilst there are many very good Bible studies and commentaries available, these can be quite off-putting for very busy people.

The studies do not claim to be an in-depth look at a particular book of the Bible. They are meant to be used as an overview and to help the reader obtain a good grasp of the subject matter without having to use hours of their time.

At the date of publication of this study the following studies are available in the BSBP series:- Ruth and Esther; Job; Hosea; Nahum, Habakkuk and Zephaniah; The Gospel of John; 1 Corinthians; James; Hebrews; Revelation Part 1 and Revelation Part 2.

Full details of all the books in both the **'How do I know?'** and the **BSBP series** can be found on the following websites. The books are all available from Amazon and selected bookstores.

http://www.howdoiknowbooks.com

https://www.amazon.com/author/margaretweston

Milton Keynes UK
Ingram Content Group UK Ltd.
UKHW011315120324
439381UK00009B/582